W9-BDH-497

INDY 500
THE INSIDE TRACK

by Nancy Roe Pimm

Published by Darby Creek Publishing,
a division of Oxford Resources, Inc.
7858 Industrial Parkway
Plain City, OH 43064
www.darbycreekpublishing.com

Text copyright © 2004 by Nancy Roe Pimm
Illustrations © 2004 by Darby Creek Publishing
Design by Keith Van Norman

Cataloging-in-Publication

Pimm, Nancy Roe.
Indy 500 : the inside track / by Nancy Roe
Pimm.
        p. ; cm.
ISBN 1-58196-021-2 hardcover
ISBN 1-58196-023-9 softcover
Summary: A look at the history and excitement
of "the Crown Jewel" of auto racing, the
Indianapolis 500, including the history of the
Indianapolis Motor Speedway and the develop-
ment of "Indy cars."—Includes bibliographical
references (p.) and index.
1. Indianapolis Speedway Race—Juvenile litera-
ture. 2. Automobile racing—Indiana—
Indianapolis—Juvenile literature. [1. Indianapolis
Speedway Race. 2. Automobile racing—
Indiana—Indianapolis. 3. Indy cars.] I. Title.
GV1033.5.I55 P56 2004
796.72/06/877252 dc22
OCLC: 54012992

Printed in the United States of America

First printing

2 4 6 8 10 9 7 5 3 1

Every year the Borg-Warner Trophy is awarded to the newest Indy 500 champion. Each winner's face, name, and winning year are permanently placed on it. The trophy also features a 24-karat-gold portrait of the late Speedway owner, Anton "Tony" Hulman. An 18-inch replica, a "Baby Borg," is given each year to the Indy 500 champion and the car owner.

TABLE OF CONTENTS

Every May, drivers from all over the world come to Indianapolis, Indiana, to test their skills. Their race cars know no nationality, race, or gender. They will go as fast as they are pushed to go. Every team races by the same rules: The car must be sixteen feet long and six-feet, six-and-a-half-inches wide. It must weigh at least 1,525 pounds, not counting the fuel or the driver.

Each driver puts on his or her race face. Calculating eyes peering through helmet, showing steely determination. Strapped into a rocket-like car, the driver is about to travel at speeds of more than 200 miles per hour, just inches off the ground with cement walls looming beside him.

The drivers line up three cars wide and eleven rows deep. After a lifetime of dreams and a month of intense preparation, the next Indy 500 champion will be decided in one afternoon. The drivers await a single command:

"Lady and gentlemen, start your engines!"

Buddy Rice, 2004

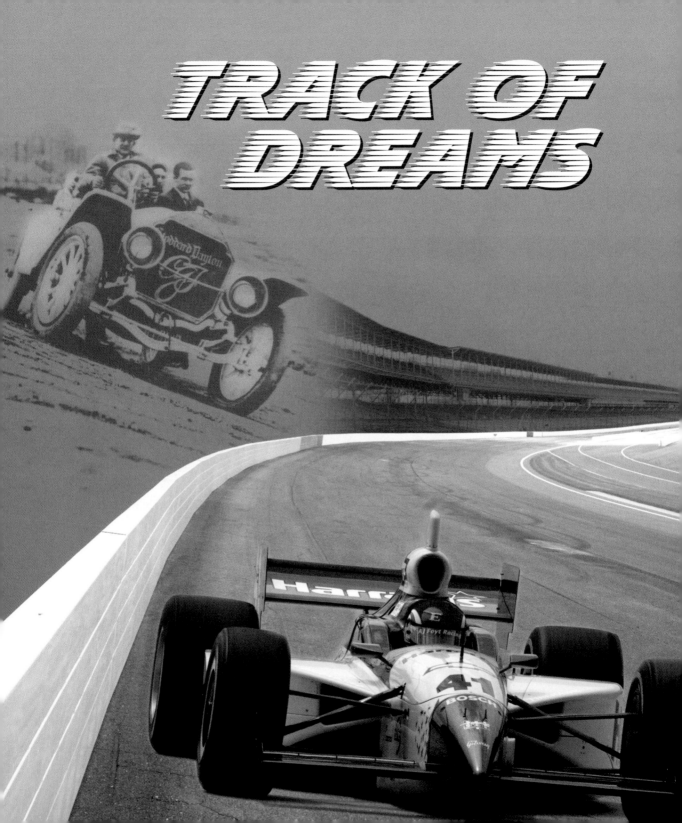

TRACK OF DREAMS

In the early 1900s, former racecar driver Carl Fisher had visions of building a test track. Along with three partners—Arthur Newby, Frank Wheeler, and Jim Allison—Mr. Fisher bought 320 acres of overgrown farmland northwest of Indianapolis, Indiana. In those days, Indianapolis—not Detroit—was "Motor City." Construction of the track began in February 1909.

By August 1909, Fisher's dream came true. A 2.5-mile, oval-shaped racetrack stood where there once had been only a cornfield. Four banked corners connected two long straightaways (5/8 mile each) and two short straightaways (1/8 mile each). The partners named their track of dreams the Indianapolis Motor Speedway.

The first race was set for August 19, 1909. Racecar drivers from all over the country came to test their cars and compete against each other

Winter 1909: Lewis Strang, who would become the pole-sitter in the 1911 Indy 500, checks out a model of the soon-to-be-constructed track.

(left to right) Tom Kincade #6, Charlie Merz #7, and William Borque #3
at the start of the track's first race on August 19, 1909.

that day. The tires on the "high-speed" cars tore up the track's crushed stone and tar surface. Five people died because of the poor track conditions.

Fisher decided to have the track repaved before opening for another race. Two months later, 3.2 million ten-pound bricks had been laid, held together with cement. Since then, the Indianapolis Motor Speedway has been known throughout the world as "the Brickyard." In 1911 the first Indy 500 was held.

The racecars kept getting faster and faster. The cars hammered away at the bricks, and they eventually broke apart, too. At first the Speedway workers patched the spots that needed repair. By the 1930s, most of the track needed to be covered with blacktop. The track was completely covered in October 1961, after the race's 50th anniversary. A 36-inch strip of bricks was left uncovered at the start/finish line, just to remind everyone how the nickname "Brickyard" began.

Tony Hulman (left), with Ray Harroun, 1911 Winner (right) on the "yard of bricks," celebrates the 50-year anniversary in 1961.

THE RACE

In 1909 and 1910, several short races were held at the "Brickyard." But in 1911, the Speedway became the home of only one race a year: The Indianapolis 500.

The first Indianapolis 500 was held on Memorial Day, May 30, 1911. Forty-six drivers from the United States and Europe came to compete for a purse of $27,550. Ninety thousand fans poured into the grandstands. They cheered on the forty drivers who had qualified for the big race.

The cars lined up in eight rows of five across. At the drop of the flag, the drivers took off and circled the track two hundred times.

When the race was over, the winner's car had averaged 74.6 miles per hour. It took more than seven hours for all of the cars to finish the race!

First race at the Indianapolis Motor Speedway, 1909

Since that day, the Indianapolis 500 has become the Super Bowl of auto racing. On each Memorial Day weekend, between 300,000 and 350,000 fans spill through the gates. More than 325 million households watch the race on television all over the world. The Indy 500 boasts the largest crowds of any single sporting event in the world.

Preparations for the race begin the first weekend of May, when the race teams pull into the track. They spend the month taking practice laps and getting ready to qualify for the race. The

INDY 500 FAST FACTS

- The slowest average speed was 74.602 mph. (Harroun, 1911)
- The fastest average speed was 185.981 mph. (Luyendyk, 2000)
- Indy-style cars accelerate from 0 to 100 mph in 3 seconds.
- Every time an Indy driver blinks, he misses 50 feet of track.
- The youngest winner was Troy Ruttman, age 22 years, 80 days. (1952)
- The oldest winner was Al Unser, age 47 years, 360 days. (1987)
- A front tire for an Indy-style car weighs about 18 lbs.
- Some drivers and fans believe that eating peanuts at the track is bad luck.

two weekends before the race, drivers must qualify their cars in time trials.

Each car entered is allowed up to three attempts to qualify. On each successful qualifying try, the driver completes four laps at top speed. The track officials calculate the average speed of the four laps. The fastest thirty-three cars qualify to race in the Indy 500. The fastest car on the first day of time trials earns the "best" position: the inside of the first row. This is called "pole position."

On race day, the drivers line up their cars in eleven rows with three cars in each row. The Indy 500 is ready to begin!

THE CROWN JEWEL OF AUTO RACING

"The Indy 500 is more important than any other race. It's full of history and tradition. It's most definitely the crown jewel of auto racing, much like the Kentucky Derby is the crown jewel of horse racing. Qualifying at Indianapolis is one of the hardest things. There is more pressure in those four laps than any other four laps you'll do the whole month."

—Bobby Rahal
1986 Indy 500 winner;
average speed: 170.722 m.p.h.

THE 2004 INDY 500 PACE CAR

Since 1979, a pace car has always led the field at the beginning of the Indy 500 race. It is the job of the pace car to control the start of the race. The officials send the pace car onto the track whenever there is a yellow (caution) flag. The pace car picks up the current leader of the race to prepare the field for a restart, when the green flag is dropped. In recent years, a retired racecar driver or a celebrity has driven the pace car.

Overhead, fighter planes fly and fireworks burst and hundreds of balloons are released. The huge crowd comes to its feet for the song, "God Bless America." The lonely sound of "Taps" hushes the masses of people. The National Anthem and "Back Home Again in Indiana" are sung. As the last note fades, the drivers listen anxiously for the command: "Lady and gentlemen, start your engines!"

Thirty-three engines roar behind the pace car as the Indy-style cars roll down the track. The drivers wave to their fans during the two parade laps. They zig-zag their cars over the pavement to warm up their tires. On the third lap—the pace lap—the cars pick up speed. It's time to get down to business. The drivers await the signal from the starter, perched high above the track. The green flag waves wildly and the race is on!

The cars scream into the first turn, ducking and diving. Five hundred miles later, when the first car passes under the checkered flag, the race is over. Then comes the celebration. The winning driver chugs the traditional drink—milk. A large wreath is placed around his neck. A new Indianapolis 500 winner is crowned.

THE DRINK OF CHAMPIONS

2003 Winner Gil de Ferran

Louis Meyer's mom once told him that milk was the most refreshing drink of all. After Louie won the 1936 Indy 500, he celebrated in the winner's circle by drinking—not champagne—but a bottle of buttermilk! To this day, the milk-drinking tradition continues at Indy.

THE CARS

George Robson, 1946

Ray Crawford, 1959

A.J. Foyt IV, 2003

In the early 1900s, the Indy racecars looked like farm tractors with tall, narrow tires. They were made of rigid steel frames covered by heavy sheet-metal bodies. The two-seater, front-engine machines had to weigh at least 2,300 pounds. The skies filled with smoke as noisy engines powered the heavy racecars through the turns and down the straightaways.

The two-seater cars held a driver and a riding mechanic. The mechanic's job was to keep the car running and to watch for passing traffic. Ray Harroun was the only driver in the first Indy 500 to drive without a mechanic. He designed a single-seater racecar and kept track of his pursuers with the use of a mirror mounted in front of the steering wheel on the body of the car. This is the first recorded use of a rearview mirror.

rearview mirror →

Ray Harroun's
1911 "Marmon Wasp"

Harroun was ahead of his time. The car he designed was also lighter and narrower than the other Indy cars in 1911. It had a hornet-like tail that earned it the nickname, "the Marmon Wasp." Ray Harroun and the Marmon Wasp won the first Indy 500. The following year, in 1912, a new rule made it mandatory to have a mechanic ride with the driver. Single-seater cars didn't become legal again until 1923.

Jules Goux, the winner of the 1913 Indy 500. Car weight: 2200 lbs. Average race speed: 75.933 mph

It wasn't long before the car builders discovered that the lighter the car, the faster the car. The rearview mirror became standard on the lighter single-seater cars. Instead of using street cars, special lightweight racecars were made for competition. Over the years the Indy-style cars have been made of steel, aluminum, carbon, or a combination of these. Today they have a carbon chassis and carbon body work. ("Indy cars" is a nickname given to the style of cars driven at the Indianapolis 500.) They became so light and fast that the drivers had trouble keeping them under control. At high speeds, the cars tended to lift off the track!

Juan Montoya, winner of the 2000 Indianapolis 500. Car weight: 1550 lbs. Average race speed: 167.607 mph

In 1971, a new design showed up among the race teams. The new Indy-style cars had two sets of wings: a set in front on the nose of the car and a large wing on the rear.

By 1979 engineers created cars that used a suction called "ground effects." Air flows by the front wings and into the tunnels underneath the car to hold the front end down. The suction that is created this way makes a 1,550-pound car hug the ground like a 3,875-pound car. Someone could actually drive one of these cars on a ceiling! At a street race in Detroit, the Indy-style cars sucked up the manhole covers as they raced over them!

The rear wing of the racecar is like an upside-down airplane wing. Instead of creating lift as on an airplane, the wing pushes the

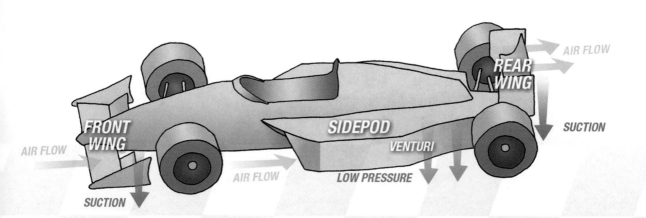

Today's Indy-style cars can travel the length of a football field in less than one second!

car down onto the track. This is called "downforce," like when a person's hand pushes down on a toy car. The air is forced up and over the racecar, which is called "aerodynamics." The wings give the drivers more control of the car. The faster the car travels, the tighter it hugs the track. The drivers rocket through the turns so fast that it almost seems as if they're flying!

Indy champ Bobby Rahal says, "The easiest laps I ever did at Indy were the fastest laps I ever did at Indy The faster you go, the better it feels. I've been in cars going slower around Indy and it scared the daylights out of me. I was on the edge, skating around for the entire lap."

THE ENGINE

The heart of the racecar is the engine. If it stops ticking, the race is over. Today most Indy-style cars are powered by an 8-cylinder, 3.0-liter methanol-fueled engine. It produces more than 675 horsepower, about four times the horsepower of a street car. Driving an Indy car around only one lap of the Brickyard (2.5 miles) is as hard on the engine as going five hundred miles in a passenger car.

Street car engines run at 2,500 to 3,500 r.p.m. (revolutions per minute). An Indy-style car runs at 10,300 r.p.m. Each piston pumps up and down at a rate of about one mile a minute. This makes a

Working on Sam Hornish's engine.

Before World War II, Indy racers drove front-engine cars. After some experimentation—and a lot of trial and error—race teams in the 1960s gradually switched to cars with rear engines. Putting the engine in the rear gave the car more balance, so it was easier to handle. This also allowed the front of the car to be smaller and nar-rower, making the entire car more aerodynamic—and faster.

An Indy 500 car team will go through an average of four engines for each car during the month of May. The engine needs to be rebuilt every 550 miles. It takes an Indy crew about one hour to change an engine.

Fuel intake, called a "buckeye"

Gasoline was used for many years, but it is very flammable. When Dave MacDonald's car hit a wall during the 1964 Indianapolis 500, the gas tank exploded, causing a fatal, fiery crash. As a result, the use of gasoline was outlawed.

race engine use a lot of fuel. An Indy-style car engine gets two miles to the gallon. It can burn two gallons of fuel per minute! One lap around the Speedway uses about 1.3 gallons of fuel, which today is methanol, not gasoline.

Methanol is an alcohol-based fuel that is less flammable than gasoline. The only problem with using methanol is that its flame is invisible. The crew can feel the heat but can't see the flame. Instead, they hear the fuel ignite, much like the sound of a gas grill starting. Buckets of water are kept in the pits in case of an accidental fire.

The tank of an Indy-style car is called a fuel cell. It holds 30 gallons of fuel and is located between the driver and the engine. A strong fuel cell is needed to keep down the threat of fire. The fuel cell is similar to the ones used in military helicopters. It is so strong that it can withstand machine-gun fire.

Each Indy 500 car team is allotted 245 gallons of methanol before the start of the race. If a team uses more than the allotted 245 gallons, the car will run out of fuel and won't be able to finish the race. That is no way to lose!

THE ROAR OF THE ENGINE

The fuel cell is the only thing between the driver's head and the engine. In Ed Pimm's first Indianapolis 500 in 1985, he forgot to put in his earplugs. For more than three hours, the engine screamed in his ears. After the race, he was nearly deaf.

"I got caught up in all the pre-race excitement," says Ed Pimm. "Before I knew it, we were called to our cars. When the green flag dropped and I stood on the throttle, I realized my earplugs were in my pocket. No way was I going to pit just for earplugs! I knew right then that I would have to spend the next 500 miles with this incredible high-pitched whining sound in my ears."

THE TIRES

Today's racing tires don't look like the first Indy 500 tires. Back in 1911, the racing tires were very skinny, like bicycle tires. They were made of cotton cords covered with a layer of rubber. Blowouts were common—and very dangerous.

Over time, racing tires changed. They became safer and helped racers drive faster. Race teams found that the wider the tire, the more grip the racecar had. When a car has grip, its wheels stay in good contact with the track's surface. Drivers have more control, especially around the turns. Compared to regular tires, racing tires need to provide more traction and grip, so they have to be softer than tires on passenger cars.

Indy-style racing tires look as if they have no tread. They look smooth and bald, so they are called "slicks." Slicks do have tread, but it is flat, not grooved. These tires only work well on dry surfaces. If it rains before or during the Indy 500, the race is postponed until the track is dry.

Tires before the race

patch
(area that touches the track)

Another factor for good tire grip is heat. When racing tires are heated up, they become sticky like chewing gum. The racecars weave back and forth across the track while waiting for the race to start to make the tires hotter. Then they will stick to the track surface better.

Heat can also be an enemy of the tire. Tire engineers and racing teams work very hard to find a tire that is soft enough to produce lots of traction without blistering or overheating. A tire that swells and pops at over 200 m.p.h. will spell D-I-S-A-S-T-E-R. Tire companies test their tires for durability in laboratories, and they pay drivers per mile to test their products on the racetrack.

Pit area with tire "peel out" marks.

INDY TIRE TRIVIA

These facts will get your wheels turning!

- The tread on an IndyCar Series tire is only slightly thicker than a credit card, 3/32nd of an inch thick.
- The front tire of one of these cars weighs about 18 pounds.
- The temperature of the tread at top speed is almost 212 degrees Farenheit—the boiling point of water.
- At 220 m.p.h. the front tires rotate about 43 times per second.
- The sticking of the tire to the track's surface is called **bite**.
- Bubbles, called **blisters**, sometimes form on the surface of the tire when the tread is overheated.
- To race faster, the drivers use the same groove around the track, which becomes darker because of rubber buildup. The dark area is called the **racing line**. Pieces of rubber get thrown off the tires and collect above the racing line. These are known as **marbles**.
- "Stickers" is a slang term for new tires that still have the manufacturer's stickers on them.
- At the Indy 500, each race team is given 35 sets of tires (140 tires) per team.
- Each tire costs about $300.
- The race teams fill their tires with nitrogen because it doesn't expand or contract as much as oxygen.
- Outer tires (on the right side) are taller than inner tires to give more control through tight turns.
- The actual amount of surface area that the tire's tread touches is called the **tire patch.**

THE COCKPIT

To step into his office, an Indy 500 driver doesn't have to open any doors. He slides into the cockpit opening, a small 36-by-19-inch area in the middle of the racecar. Mario Andretti says, "When they made the call, 'Drivers, to your cars!' it was such a relief. My racecar was my

Mario Andretti

office. It was the place where I felt most relaxed. I had no distractions, and I could be totally focused. I could hardly wait for the green flag to drop so I could get down to business."

The cockpit is so small that teams need to unhook the steering wheel and the headrest in order for the driver to fit. Once the driver is seated, he or she is hooked into place. The driver's seat is an exact mold of his or her body. The racer fits so snugly in the cockpit that a crewmember has to buckle the driver's seatbelt for him. A cockpit is also known as "the tub" or the monocoque. It is made of carbon fiber. This is the same material NASA uses for building rockets in its space program. It also contains Kevlar©, a material

Inside the Cheever Indy-style race car cockpit

used in bullet-proof vests, making the cockpit super-strong to protect the driver.

The long, narrow front of the car is called the nose. Behind the nose and the front tires is the footwell. The gas pedal, brake pedal, clutch pedal, and foot rest are here. The foot rest is a "dead" pedal, used for support around the turns or as a place for the driver to rest his or her foot. Under the driver's legs is a fire extinguisher. One push of a button releases the chemical to put out a fire.

Once the driver is strapped inside the car, he doesn't use a key to start the engine. A crewmember fits the end of a starter into the crankshaft at the rear of the racecar. The starter turns the engine in the same way that a hand-crank did on the Model T Fords.

Buddy Rice nestled in the cockpit, 2004.

Unlike a street car with gauges on the dashboard, the Indy-style car has its gauges on the steering wheel. It displays the oil and water temperatures, tire pressures, and the revolutions per minute (r.p.m.s) of the engine. The driver even has an overtake button, which

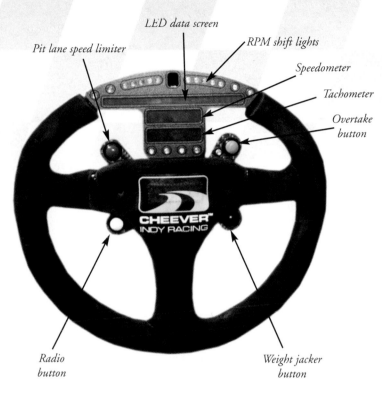

Pit lane speed limiter

LED data screen

RPM shift lights

Speedometer

Tachometer

Overtake button

Radio button

Weight jacker button

gives the engine more fuel. This gives the car more horsepower to help the driver pass another car. A cruise control button limits the car's speed in the pits to only 60 m.p.h.!

The gearshift in an Indy-style car is similar to that of a motorcycle. The driver simply uses his hand to pull the shifter up when he or she wants to go up a gear—and pushes it down to drop into a lower gear.

wind tunnel test

An Indy car has no roof, so the cockpit is open. The driver must wear a special helmet that not only protects his or her head, but also aerodynamically cuts through the air. At high speeds, a driver used to feel an upward pull of more than fifty pounds on his helmet. The helmet shook violently from side to side, straining the driver's neck muscles and, at times, causing blurred vision. Engineers studied the helmets in wind tunnels, using yarn tufts taped to the helmet and smoke to watch the airflow. The thickly padded helmet they created has a diffuser in the back and a chin spoiler in the front, both making the air run smoothly over the surface of the helmet. The driver has less neck fatigue and fewer vision problems.

Directly behind the driver's head is an air intake opening called an airbox. Air travels into the airbox and is forced into the engine. The rollbar that protects the driver's head is built into the airbox. The Indy car is not just built for speed—it also has to be one of the safest cars ever made.

airbox

Sam Hornish, Jr.

THE DRIVER

There is more to being a driver at Indy than just getting behind the wheel and taking off. Before a driver can race in the Indianapolis 500, he or she must pass a rookie test. It is made of four different ten-lap segments. Most drivers who make it this far have already won a championship in another series, such as the Infinity Pro Series (formula cars), Formula Atlantic, or midget or sprint car series.

Champions from all over the world, from all forms of racing, come to test their skills at the Indy 500.

Racecar drivers push their cars—and their bodies—to the limit. Their goal is to drive as fast as they can without crashing. Reaching speeds of 240 miles per hour increases the pull of gravity by four to five times. That means that a 170-pound man will feel as if he weighs 680 pounds! It is the same amount of force an astronaut feels during take off in a space shuttle. The pull is so strong that the Indy Racing League recommends that an Indy 500 driver should use the HANS (Head And Neck System) safety device.

HANS device

The helmet has a built-in straw for drinking during the long, hot race. A two-way radio inside the helmet keeps the driver in constant contact with his or her crews.

WILBUR SHAW: FACING THE FEAR

After his first Indy 500 in 1927, Wilbur Shaw told people, "I felt I had been sucked into a hundred-mile-an-hour tornado. I was never so scared in my life." Scared or not, Wilbur Shaw went on to win the Indy 500 three times!

The driver has to be physically and mentally fit. Most drivers work out every day and keep themselves on special diets. At rest a driver has a normal heart rate of about 60 beats per minute. But while the driver is racing, his or her heart rate may reach 170 to 190 beats per minute—for three to four hours! This is similar to the heart rate of a marathon runner.

The physical needs of a driver include his or her clothing. The drivers wear fireproof long underwear made of Nomex®. Over the Nomex® they wear a quilted jumpsuit, which is also fireproof. Drivers wear thick gloves and a ski-mask-like hood, both made of Nomex®. Then they strap on a helmet and are belted into the cockpit, where the temperatures can reach 120 to 150 degrees Fahrenheit. By the time the checkered flag drops to end the race, a driver will lose six percent of his or her total body weight due to dehydration. For a 170-pound man, that is about 10 pounds of sweat!

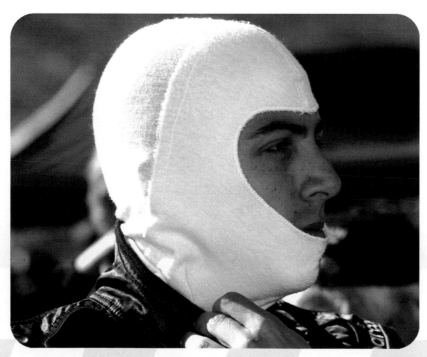

NOMEX® ski mask

Jeff Ward gets a little hep from his pit crew.

Contrary to some people's beliefs, the race driver does not have a "death wish." He or she must be mentally and emotionally stable. A driver must remain calm during life-threatening situations. Racing can be dangerous, so drivers must have a clear mind and logical thinking in order to survive. Like most champions, drivers are usually competitive, assertive, persistent, and very intelligent.

WOMEN DRIVERS

Janet Guthrie

Lyn St. James

Sarah Fisher

For years, the "women of Indy" were the wives of the drivers and crewmembers. In 1977, **Janet Guthrie** changed that. She became the first woman to qualify for the Indianapolis 500. **Lyn St. James** followed in her tire prints in 1992, finishing eleventh in her first year and earning the title of Rookie of the Year. She raced in every Indy 500 from 1992 to 1997. In 2000, **Sarah Fisher** qualified and in May 2002, she became the fastest female qualifier at Indy, with a four-lap average speed of more than 229 miles per hour!

Today, more girls than ever are soapbox derby competitors, quarter midget racers, junior dragsters, and go-kart racers. As these girls explore the training grounds of auto racing, it is likely that more women will qualify for the world's greatest race— the Indianapolis 500.

Quarter midget racer

HOW CAN DRIVERS AFFORD TO RACE?

It takes a lot of money to run an Indy-style car. The race teams rely on sponsors. The sponsors pay to have their product's name on the cars, on driver's suits, on team uniforms, and on transporters.

The cost of an Indy-style car can be more than $300,000. Each driver needs at least two. The wheels of an Indy-style car cost $2,000 apiece. A team needs about ten sets of wheels for each car. Most cars need six engines to get through the month, at a cost of $125,000 each. Even the steering wheel costs $60,000! Transporters get the cars to the races. These big rigs can cost close to $400,000.

How much does it cost to run a racecar in the Indy 500?

One driver in **one** car for **one** month costs about **1 million to 1.5 million dollars!**

transporter

THE PIT STOP

The Indy 500 race is not only on the track—it is also in the pits. The pits are located beside the front straightaway of the track. Each driver is assigned a pit area. During the race, the mechanics, tires, spare

tire swap in the pits

parts, and fuel (methanol) are kept in the pits.

The crew chief watches from behind the pit wall. He talks with the driver by using a two-way radio. In the first Indy 500 in 1911, a riding mechanic rode with the driver.

The cars zip into the pits to refuel, change tires, and make repairs. Teams strive to complete their pit stop in less than eleven seconds. Each team is allowed to have six men over the pit wall to work on the car: four men for tires, one for fuel, and one for the air jack that lifts the car up.

Sam Hornish, Jr. takes a pit stop.

PIT STOP SEQUENCE: BUDDY RICE, MAY 30, 2004

1 Pit crew members signals driver in. Tires and air wrench are in place.

2 The car pulls into the pits. The air jack man scrambles over the wall and inserts an air hose in a fitting at the top of the car. The compressed air pressurizes the jacks to lift the car up off the ground.

3 He then inserts a vent in the top of the fuel cell to let the air escape, allowing the gas to go in faster.

4 Meanwhile, the fueler puts the fuel hose into an opening called a "buckeye."

5 While the fuel flows, the four tire men sprint to their stations. The wail of impact wrenches pierces the air as they spin the one and only lug nut off each wheel.

6 Crewmembers behind the wall take away the old wheels and hand over new ones.

7 Air wrenches are reversed and the new wheels are tightened into place.

8 Two tire men check the side-pod vents for obstructions while the other two check the wings.

9 The fueler disconnects the hose and the fuel cell automatically seals itself. Hoses are handed to the crew back over the wall.

10 The air jack man releases the jack, and the car falls to the ground.

11 Crewmembers stand behind the car, ready to give it a push if it stalls.

12 One crewmember by the outside front tire sees all is clear and signals the driver to GO-GO-GO!

The driver—and his newly tired and fueled car—hit the track and rejoin the race.
All in less than twelve seconds!

The most successful pit crew of the Indy 500 is the Penske racing team. To stay in tune with each other, the Penske team practices several times a month, year-round. Through the years, the team has earned 13 wins and 12 pole positions, more than any other team in history. The Penske team dominated the 500 five times, winning the pole position and the race. Out of the eighteen different men who drove for Penske, nine of them became Indianapolis 500 winners.

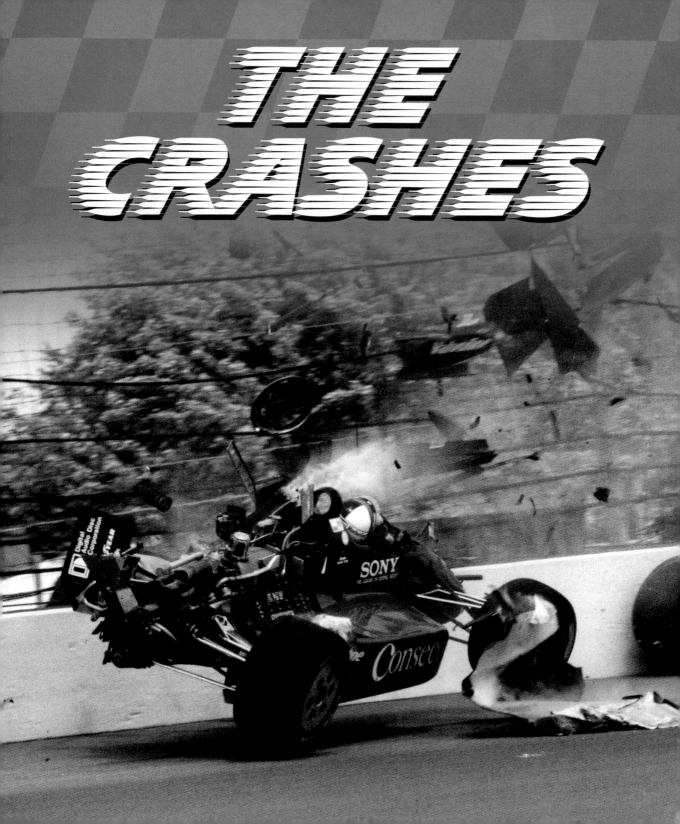

THE CRASHES

How do so many drivers walk away from 200-mph crashes? Indy style cars are made to be safe at top speeds. The bodywork absorbs the impact of the crash before it gets to the driver. Parts of the car break off on impact. The driver's feet are protected because they are located behind the front wheels of the car. A six-point safety harness holds the driver tightly inside the cockpit. It has a quick-release buckle to allow him or her to escape quickly. The HANS (head and neck system) fastened to the helmet keeps the driver's head from shooting forward in a sudden stop, reducing neck injuries. And the driver's flame-resistant clothing just might come in handy if the car bursts into flames.

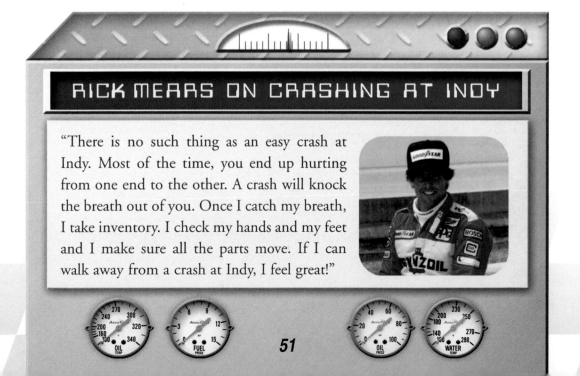

RICK MEARS ON CRASHING AT INDY

"There is no such thing as an easy crash at Indy. Most of the time, you end up hurting from one end to the other. A crash will knock the breath out of you. Once I catch my breath, I take inventory. I check my hands and my feet and I make sure all the parts move. If I can walk away from a crash at Indy, I feel great!"

Johnny Rutherford, 1988

INSIDE AN INDY CRASH

The Indy car driver straps his helmet into place and pulls on his fireproof gloves. He lowers himself into the cockpit of his sleek racing machine. It is qualifying day at the Indianapolis 500 and winning the pole position would be a dream come true. His job is to find the fastest way around the two and a half mile oval, for four consecutive laps. A crewmember buckles up his safety harness. The driver pops the steering wheel into place. The starter is engaged, and the engine roars. The driver slaps the car into gear and cruises down the pit lane.

On the warm-up lap, the driver tests his car. He listens for any sounds of trouble. He feels every little movement and every little bump through the seat of his pants. To warm up the tires, he weaves back and forth on the track. The car feels good! All systems are go. It's time to bring the car up to speed.

He completes the first lap going full speed without needing to brake. The engine is screaming as the car rockets down the straightaway in front of the grandstand, reaching a speed of more than 200 miles per hour.

Once again, he soars through the first turn. As he enters the second turn, a sudden gust of wind pushes the car off the racing line. The rear of the car loses its grip, causing it

A.J. Foyt IV hits the wall.

to drift and veer toward the wall. The driver knows the car has passed the point of no return. This spin can't be saved! The wall is coming at him—and then it's gone. He's headed for the wall again—and then it's gone. He knows he has no choice but to go along for the ride—a wild ride. He is on a rollercoaster without tracks, launched into the unknown.

With no hope of avoiding the crash, the driver realizes it's time for "turtle mode." He lets go of the steering wheel and pulls his arms to his sides. He knows that if he hangs onto the steering wheel, the impact of the crash could shatter his wrists. He puts his head down and closes his eyes.

Spectators see the car slam into the wall while skidding down the track backwards. The sound of metal scraping the concrete barrier pierces the air. The tires are screeching, and the air smells of burning rubber. The car is breaking into pieces around the driver. Sheet metal drags down the track behind the crumbled car. Then suddenly the driver feels as if he were shot out of a cannon into a concrete wall. His head shakes back and forth inside his helmet, like a clapper inside a ringing bell. Everything goes black. The wall has delivered the knockout punch.

Seconds later, he opens his eyes. The force of the impact is so great that he cannot move, he cannot speak, and he can hardly breathe. He tries to force air down into his lungs, but heaviness settles on his chest and his lungs tighten. The car finally stops. Although his vision is blurred, he takes inventory of all his body parts. He wiggles his hands and feet to make certain they move.

Johnny Rutherford, 1988

The safety crew is already at his side. With fire extinguishers ready for action, they unbuckle the safety harness and pull the stunned driver out of the car. The driver is helped into the ambulance to be taken to the trackside hospital. He must see the doctor before he can be released to get back into the race in his back-up car.

He knows that soon he will be hurting all over, but for the moment, he feels great. He knows he is a lucky man. He has survived a crash at the Indianapolis 500.

KENNY BRACK CRASHES IN 1999

Winner of the 1999 Indy 500, Kenny Brack survived one of the worst crashes in Indy car history in 2003 at the Texas Motor Speedway. The accident recorded 200 G-forces, meaning he felt the pressure of 200 times his own body weight on impact. "At the end of the crash," says Brack, "everything broke off the car, absorbing the impact. But my cockpit was intact. Nothing penetrated it. It probably saved my life. My crash was a testament to how safe these cars are."

THE FLAGS

The checkered flag has been waved at the Indy 500 since the first race in 1911. Since then, other flags have been added to let the drivers know about the condition of the track and the flow of the race. The flags are used during practice, qualifying, and the race itself, to keep the race as safe as possible and to enforce regulations. Even with all the high-tech radios, computers, and spotters, the flags are a good way to "talk" to the drivers during the noisy racing action. The flags tell the drivers important things, like "Slow down," "Stop! The track is unsafe!" or "One lap to go!" The checkered flag means "The End!"

The checkered flags mark the end of the race.

LAPS AND LAPTOPS

Computers have invaded the world of Indy cars. Engineer Walter Preston of Team Rahal says, "Laptops and flat screens—you can't live without them anymore. It's a total video game." The drivers and crews rely on the Pi data retrieving system, hidden in the car's sidepod. It gathers information through sensors on the cars and transmitters on the track. The Pi box is "the brains" of the racecar. It records and calculates everything from fuel mileage, G forces, lap time, lap speed, corner speeds, oil temperatures, tire pressures, gear ratios, ride height, and much, much more. It "talks" to the driver through an LED (Light Emitting Diodes) display on the steering wheel. The pit crew and the driver use the data to make decisions and adjustments about the car and their race strategy.

GREEN
Start! Go!

This flag is used to start the race or to restart the race after a yellow or red flag.

YELLOW
Caution!

Conditions are unsafe. Slow down and keep your position. Passing is not allowed while the yellow flag is out. Cars can bunch up single-file. The yellow flag comes out for debris on the track, an oil spill, or an accident. Drivers must yield to track safety vehicles.

BLACK
Into the pits!

The driver who gets the black flag must take his car into the pits immediately.

BLUE WITH DIAGONAL ORANGE STRIPE
Let them pass!
The slower cars must allow the faster cars to pass.

RED
Stop!
The race is stopped because it is unsafe to continue racing.

WHITE
One lap left!
This flag is waved when the leader has only one lap left of his 500-mile race.

BLACK-AND-WHITE CHECKERED
The race is over!
The first car shown the black-and-white checkered flag is the winner.

SO, YOU WANT TO BE AN INDY DRIVER . . .

Did you know that you can start your racing career as early as age five? Racing go-karts is a great training ground for future Indy car drivers. Karting is offered on dirt tracks, paved tracks, oval tracks, or road courses. Purchasing a kart of your own costs about $2,000 to $5,000. Karting schools offer rentals from $25.00 to $500.00. "The younger you start, the better. The best way to get ready to drive bigger cars is to start with go-karts," says former go-kart racer and 2004 Indy 500 Winner Buddy Rice. Some series available to 15- to 20-year-olds moving through the ranks are the Formula Ford, Formula Barber Dodge, Formula Mazda, and the Formula BMW. The steppingstone to the Indy Racing League is the Infinity Pro Series. Once you get there, you could be just one step away from racing at Indy!

BUDDY RICE

2004 Indy 500 Winner

"Buy a kart, invest in tires and gas, and go racing!"

ACKNOWLEDGMENTS

I want to thank many special people for helping make this book possible: my friend John Anderson, for sharing his knowledge and expertise in the field of auto racing; Jim Trueman, Mike Curb, and Patrick Kehoe for believing in my husband, Ed Pimm, and helping to make his dream of racing in the Indy 500 come true; Rick Mears, Bobby Rahal, Ed Pimm, Mario Andretti, Kenny Brack, Buddy Rice, and Lyn St. James for sharing their memories and stories with me. You've made me discover that auto racing is not for the faint of heart. You are true warriors! Thanks, too, to Rahal Letterman Racing for all their help, especially Bill VandeSandt, Linda Lett, Donna Filson, Walter Preston, and Scott Roembke.

Heartfelt thanks also go to Stephanie Greene for being the best cheerleader a writer ever had, to my critique group in Columbus, Ohio—Erin MacLellan, Carol Ottolenghi, Andrea Pelleschi, and Kristi Lewis—and to my mentor, editor, and friend, Tanya Dean, for believing in me and for believing in this book.

Most of all, I'd like to thank my husband, Ed Pimm, for sharing his love of auto racing and showing me the way to follow your dreams, no matter how far-fetched they may seem.

-NRP

BIBLIOGRAPHY

Anderson, John. Senior Manager of Technology for Champ Cars, Formerly Crew Chief and Team Manager for many Indy 500 Race Teams. Interview: August 2002.

Andretti, Mario. 1969 Indianapolis 500 Winner; Championship Auto Racing Team Owner. Interview: September 2002.

Brack, Kenny. 1999 Indianapolis 500 Winner and driver for Team Rahal. Interview: April 2004.

Carnegie, Tom. *Indy 500—More Than a Race*. Tokyo, Japan: McGraw-Hill Book Company, [n.d.].

Dregni, Michael. *The Indianapolis 500*. Minneapolis, Minnesota: Capstone Press, 1994

Maynard, Chris. Racing Cars. London, England: Frank Watts, 1999.

Mears, Rick. Four-time Indianapolis 500 Winner: 1979, 1984, 1988, and 1991. Consultant for Team Penske. August 2003.

Popely, Rick with Spencer Riggs. *Indianapolis 500 Chronicle*. Lincolnwood, Illinois: Publications International, Ltd. 1998.

Preston, Walter. Race engineer for Team Rahal, Formula Atlantic. Interview: April 2004.

Rahal, Bobby. 1986 Indianapolis 500 Winner; Team owner: Indy Racing League, Formula Atlantic Team, Championship Auto Racing Team. Interview: September 2003.

Rice, Buddy. Driver in 2003 Indianapolis 500 for Team Rahal. Interview: April 2004.

Rubel, David. *How to Drive an Indy Race Car*. Santa Fe, New Mexico: Agincourt Press, 1992.

Savage, Jeff. *Racing Cars*. Minneapolis, Minnesota: Capstone Press, 1961.

Schwartz, Chris. Director of Marketing and Communications for Penske Racing. Interview: January 2004.

St. James, Lyn. 1992 Rookie of the Year at Indy. Second woman to qualify for the Indianapolis 500. Interview: January 2004.

Taylor, Rich. *Indy: Seventy-Five Years of Racing's Greatest Spectacle*. New York, New York: St. Martin's Press, 1991.

Weber, Bruce. *The Indianapolis 500*. Mankato, Minnesota: Creative Education, Inc., 1990.

Wukovits, John F. *The Composite Guide to Auto Racing*. Philadelphia, Pennsylvania: Chelsea House Publishers, 1999.

BIBLIOGRAPHY

http://brickyard.com/500/

The official website for the Indianapolis 500 Hall of Fame Museum. They have schedules, tickets, photos, and more.

http://www.indy500.com/stats/

Contains driver biographies, driver statistics, qualifying records, race winners, race, and all-time statistics. You can even purchase photographs of your favorite drivers.

http://www.indyracing.com/indycar/

Contains Indy Racing Series results. You can sign up for an e-newsletter, shop at a fan store, take a virtual lap around a racetrack, or check the schedule of your favorite drivers' appearances.

http://lynstjames.com

Information about the Lyn St. James Foundation, a program that mentors young females who want to race.

http://skipbarber.com

All about a school that teaches young people the art and craft of racecar driving. Also at **www.skipbarber.com/karting**, you can find out how to go from go-karts to Skip Barber school.

http://worldkarting.com

A great site for kids interested in the world of go-kart racing.

Indianapolis Motor Speedway pagoda

GLOSSARY

aerodynamics the science that deals with the effects of the car moving through air.

airflow the movement of air around the chassis of a racecar.

bite the adhesion of a tire to the track's surface.

carbon fiber a high-tech material made of fibers woven and mixed with glues. It can be formed into any shape, and then heated to make a material harder than steel.

cockpit the place in the car where a driver sits.

downforce the force that presses the car to the ground, produced by air flowing under and over the moving car.

fuel cell a container that holds methanol in a racecar, similar to a gas tank in a passenger car.

ground effects the downforce created by both the low pressure area between the underbody and the ground and the front and rear wings.

horsepower a unit for measuring an engine's power, originally based on the amount of effort a number of horses exert as they pull a load.

lap a single complete circuit of a racetrack.

methanol pure methyl alcohol that is used as fuel in all Indy Racing League IndyCar Series cars.

Nomex® the trade name for DuPont's fire-resistant fabric that is used to make protective clothing.

pits the place beside the racetrack where crews add fuel, change tires, or make repairs during a race.

pole position the position on the inside of the first row at the beginning of a race, usually awarded to the fastest car during qualifying races.

side pod bodywork on the side of the car that covers the radiators and engine exhaust. It aids in engine cooling, aerodynamics, and protection of the driver during a side impact.

slicks smooth tires used for racing on dry surfaces.

splash-and-go a pit stop in which the driver stops only for fuel.

sponsor a company or individual who provides the financial support for a race team.

time trials the four laps that the drivers take alone on the track to determine who qualifies for the Indianapolis 500. The thirty-three fastest four-lap averages qualify.

transporter a huge truck that carries the racecar and supplies to the races.

Venturi a narrow tunnel under the side pod, shaped like an inverted wing. Air through the tunnel creates low pressure or a suction effect, which holds the car to the track.